LEARN MEDIA LITERACY SKILLS

HOW TO EVALUATE
SOURCES OF INFORMATION

by Heather C. Hudak

BrightPoint Press

San Diego, CA

© 2025 BrightPoint Press
an imprint of ReferencePoint Press, Inc.
Printed in the United States

For more information, contact:
BrightPoint Press
PO Box 27779
San Diego, CA 92198
www.BrightPointPress.com

ALL RIGHTS RESERVED.
No part of this work covered by the copyright hereon may be reproduced or used in any form or by any means—graphic, electronic, or mechanical, including photocopying, recording, taping, web distribution, or information storage retrieval systems—without the written permission of the publisher.

LIBRARY OF CONGRESS CATALOGING-IN-PUBLICATION DATA

Name: Hudak, Heather C., author.
Title: How to evaluate sources of information / by Heather C. Hudak
Description: San Diego, CA: BrightPoint Press, 2025 | Series: Learn media literacy skills | Audience: Grade 7 to 9 | Includes bibliographical references and index.
Identifiers: ISBN: 9781678209742 (hardcover) | ISBN: 9781678209759 (eBook)
The complete Library of Congress record is available at www.loc.gov.

CONTENTS

AT A GLANCE   4

INTRODUCTION   6
A MOON LANDING CONSPIRACY?

CHAPTER ONE   12
FALSE INFORMATION

CHAPTER TWO   20
SOURCES OF INFORMATION

CHAPTER THREE   32
SPOTTING UNRELIABLE SOURCES

CHAPTER FOUR   46
PUTTING SOURCES TO THE TEST

Glossary   58
Source Notes   59
For Further Research   60
Index   62
Image Credits   63
About the Author   64

AT A GLANCE

- Information is everywhere. However, not everything a person reads or hears is trustworthy.

- Misinformation is false or inaccurate information that someone spreads accidentally. Disinformation is false information that is spread on purpose.

- Believing false information can cause people to make poor decisions.

- The internet helps false information spread quickly.

- Sources can be primary, secondary, or tertiary.

- Primary sources are from people who directly experienced an event, while secondary sources review information from primary sources. Tertiary sources compile information from primary and secondary sources.

- Sources provided by schools, government agencies, and charities are generally reliable. Sources with spelling errors are often unreliable.

- Some sources look legitimate but are actually unreliable. Websites and images should be carefully evaluated before being trusted.

- People can use the SIFT method to find reliable sources. The SIFT method encourages people to stop, investigate, find better coverage, and trace claims, quotes, and media back to their original context.

INTRODUCTION

A MOON LANDING CONSPIRACY?

It was 2009. Two newspapers in Bangladesh had just released a massive story. Famous astronaut Neil Armstrong had declared that the moon landing was faked. He said he had been convinced by **conspiracy theorists**. He now believed that the journey had been staged. "The entire thing was filmed on a sound stage, most likely in New Mexico," the articles quoted Armstrong as saying. "I suppose it

Neil Armstrong was the first person to walk on the moon.

really was one small step for man, one giant lie for mankind."[1]

The articles caught a lot of attention. People were stunned. But then the newspapers issued a statement. The story was made up. It had originally been written by a satire website called *The Onion*. Satire websites publish fake stories. Normally the stories make people laugh. They may

The Onion was founded in 1988.

exaggerate to point out problems with society. Satire is not meant to be taken seriously. But the Bangladesh newspapers thought the story about Armstrong was real. They translated the story into Bengali. Then they published it as fact.

"We thought it was true," said Hasanuzzaman Khan. Khan was an editor for one of the newspapers. "So we printed it without checking. We didn't know *The Onion* was not a real news site."[2]

Khan's mistake was understandable. *The Onion* has been mistaken for a reliable news source by many people. Its website looks legitimate. Its articles look similar to those from **reputable** news sources. How was Khan supposed to know that the source was unreliable?

Social media is the most popular news source for teens.

FINDING THE TRUTH

Information is everywhere. It is in newspapers and magazines. It is in books and on TV. It is on the radio and online. But much of the information people see is not true. Some of it has innocent mistakes. Other information is made up to trick people.

Media literacy can help people evaluate sources of information. Media literacy is the ability to evaluate and create media.

People with good media literacy evaluate the sources they get information from. They question the information they find. Then they verify what they learn.

It is important to know how to find trustworthy sources. This can help people find accurate information. It can also stop inaccurate information from being shared. Journalist Amanda Ruggeri says this is a responsibility that everyone shares.

"Today, anyone can make a claim on social media," Ruggeri says. "And anyone can be the person whose re-sharing of that claim is the one who makes it go viral. That means it's the responsibility of each one of us to make sure that what we are posting, liking, and sharing is, first and foremost, actually true."[3]

CHAPTER ONE

FALSE INFORMATION

There are two main types of false information. The first is misinformation. Misinformation is inaccurate information that is spread unintentionally. People sharing the information believe it to be true. They do not mean to harm others by sharing it. They simply get the facts wrong.

The second type of false information is disinformation. Disinformation is inaccurate information that is spread on purpose.

False information is common on social media.

The people sharing it know the information is not true. But they share it anyway. Disinformation is meant to mislead people.

SPREADING FALSE INFORMATION

Misinformation and disinformation are not new. People have spread false information for thousands of years. But the internet has made this easier than ever. It is a fast way

Confirmation Bias

People are more likely to believe information if it supports their beliefs. This is called confirmation **bias**. Confirmation bias may lead people to believe unreliable sources that agree with them. It might also cause people to disregard reliable information that goes against what they believe. Confirmation bias is often unintentional. But it still affects many people.

On X, false news stories are 70 percent more likely to be shared than true news stories.

to spread fake information. It allows lies to quickly spread around the world.

People often spread false information to trick others into doing something. Salespeople may spread disinformation so people buy a product. Politicians may do it to win votes. Magazines may do it to catch readers' interest.

People may also spread disinformation to create conflict. Heather Kelly is a reporter.

She says, "The groups spreading [false information] could be trying to rile up supporters or create more tension between people on opposing sides of an issue."[4]

False information can spread rapidly. People tell their friends about the information. They share it on social media. The information can quickly reach millions of people. Researchers have found that false information spreads faster than true information. This is because it is often more interesting or exciting.

EFFECTS OF FALSE INFORMATION

Sometimes false information can be harmless. Canadian airline WestJet once announced that people could purchase a one-way trip into space for $500,000

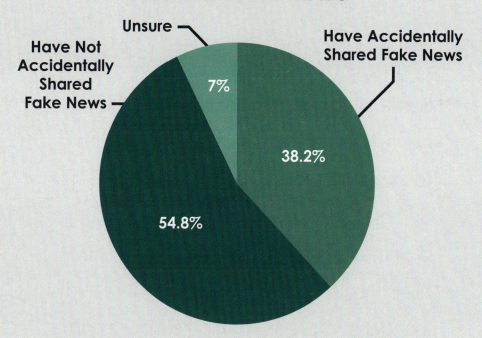

Source: Amy Watson, "Share of People Who Have Ever Accidentally Shared Fake News or Information on Social Media in the United States as of December 2020," Statista, March 21, 2023. www.statista.com.

In 2020, more than 38 percent of surveyed US adults admitted to accidentally sharing fake news on social media.

per ticket. It was later revealed as an April Fool's Day joke. It made people laugh.

Other false information can cause real harm. It can lead people to make poor decisions. This was obvious during the COVID-19 pandemic. False information was widely shared about COVID vaccines. Some social media posts claimed that the vaccines killed people. News articles reported that the vaccines caused autism. Some sources even claimed the pandemic did not exist. None of this was true. But the conspiracy theories spread. One study found that more than 57 percent of people reported seeing misinformation about COVID vaccines. The misinformation made

The World Health Organization says that vaccine hesitancy is a threat to global health.

many people hesitant to get the vaccine. This caused people to die from the virus.

Sharing false information does not affect just the person who shares the lies. It also affects everyone who sees it. These people could be friends or family members. They might even be total strangers. People must ensure that they pass along only true information.

"Individually, we may all play a small role," says Gordon Pennycook. Pennycook is a psychologist who studies misinformation at Cornell University. "But we shouldn't underestimate our collective role in improving the information ecosystem. If we aren't each doing our best to get good information out there, misinformation is going to win."[5]

CHAPTER TWO

SOURCES OF INFORMATION

It can be difficult to know if information is true or false. Looking critically at the information's source can make this easier. Evaluating a source can help determine if it is trustworthy.

There are several steps to evaluating a source. The first is determining what type of source it is. There are three types of sources. Sources can be primary, secondary, or tertiary. Understanding these

Libraries are great places to find reputable sources.

Anne Frank kept a diary during World War II (1939–1945). Because she wrote the journal about her firsthand experiences, the journal is a primary source.

categories can help people evaluate whether information is credible. It can also help people find certain types of information.

PRIMARY SOURCES

Primary sources are firsthand accounts. Some are about events. Others are about specific subjects. Primary sources are created by people who have experience with a subject. They contain eyewitness accounts. They may also contain original ideas and raw data.

Primary sources include diaries. They also include autobiographies. Primary sources can take the form of emails. They can be speeches. The sources might not even be words. Photos can be primary sources. So can paintings and other works of art.

The Information-Literate Historian is a book about researching and evaluating sources. It says,

> *Primary sources are items that are directly associated with their producer or user and the time period in which they were created. A primary source reflects the **authority** and perspective of someone who directly experienced what they are describing.*[6]

But just because a person experienced something firsthand does not mean the content they create is accurate. People experience things in different ways. What one person saw or felt might differ from what another person experienced.

A play was written about Anne Frank. It used her diary as inspiration. Because Frank did not write the play, the play is a secondary source.

Primary sources are also subjective. They reflect the creator's thoughts and feelings. They need to be evaluated carefully for bias and **validity**.

SECONDARY SOURCES

Secondary sources are created by taking information from primary sources and making something new. These sources discuss events after they occur. Secondary sources are created by people who do not have firsthand knowledge of the subject. These people **analyze** other sources of information. They do not present new information. But they may provide new analysis of existing information. Examples of secondary sources include

Reliable Authors

Written secondary sources can be useful for finding analysis of subjects. But people should make sure the secondary source is written by a reliable author. Reliable authors have backgrounds in the areas they are writing about. They may have degrees in the subjects. They may have work experience with the subjects. People should always review a person's **credentials** before trusting an author.

books and articles. They may also include biographies and documentaries.

Secondary sources are usually meant to be objective. They contain secondhand information. This means they are one step removed from the subject. But it is still important to evaluate secondary sources for bias and validity. Secondary sources may also be less reliable than primary sources.

TERTIARY SOURCES

Tertiary sources are a **consolidation** of other sources. They are thirdhand. Information is gathered from various sources. It is then summarized.

Tertiary sources do not introduce new information. They do not offer new analysis. They simply bring together information from other sources. Tertiary sources may have more than one author.

Examples of tertiary sources include dictionaries and encyclopedias. They may also include guidebooks and textbooks. These sources are not meant to be read from front to back in their entirety. They are used for reference.

SPOTTING THE DIFFERENCE

It can be difficult for people to tell what type of source they are looking at. But thinking critically about the source can help people decide. People can start by asking questions.

Readers evaluating a source can first ask if the authors personally experienced the subject. Were the authors present

An encyclopedia about World War II would likely be a tertiary source.

during the events they are writing about? Sometimes the source is an image. Did the authors take the photos themselves? If so, the source is probably primary.

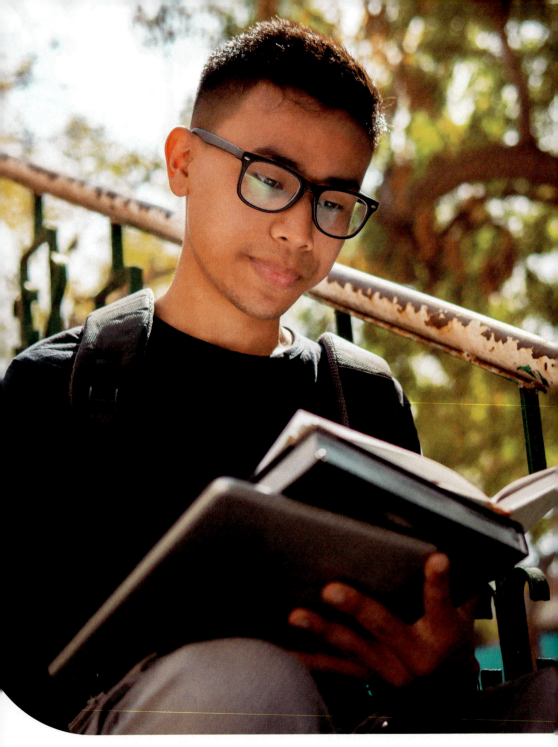

To better understand a subject, people should find information from multiple types of sources.

People can also ask how the authors know about the subject. How did they know details such as names and dates? Primary source authors know these facts from firsthand experience. Secondary and tertiary source authors will know these facts from research.

Asking questions can also help people determine if a source is secondary or tertiary. Where did the information come from? Secondary sources take information from primary sources. Tertiary sources summarize information from primary and secondary sources.

CHAPTER THREE

SPOTTING UNRELIABLE SOURCES

Misinformation is everywhere. It is more important than ever for people to know how to evaluate sources. Finding trustworthy sources is the easiest way to find reliable information. But there are many sources available. It can be difficult to determine which are legitimate. Luckily, there are clues people can look for.

Some hints can be applied to any type of source. Sources containing spelling

Learning to spot unreliable sources takes practice.

errors or grammatical mistakes are often unreliable. Reputable sources make sure their information is well-written.

Websites whose URLs end in .gov are run by the US government.

Sources that frequently post outrageous information might also be suspicious. Unreliable sources may post information to make people feel emotional. Heather Kelly says, "If something feels too outrageous or satisfying, regardless of whether it lines up with your views, pause and do more research."[7]

WEBSITES

There are specific clues that let people know that a website is reliable. Some websites are more reliable than others. Government websites and charities are typically trustworthy sources. So are research centers and schools. URLs for these sources usually end in .gov, .org, or .edu. But no matter where information comes from, it needs to be evaluated to ensure that it is credible.

Unreliable websites sometimes try to pose as credible sources. This is called website spoofing or cloning. A dangerous company may make a fake website that looks almost exactly like a trusted company's site. The sites might have the same logo. They might even have the same images. These websites often contain **malware**. Scammers use these kinds of sites to steal personal information. This information includes credit card numbers and passwords.

People can identify unreliable websites by paying close attention to details. Fake websites often have grammar and spelling errors. The websites might look outdated.

Websites designed to steal user data are known as phishing websites.

37

Sometimes the websites may have missing information. Other times the information that is there may be incorrect.

Another way to spot a fake website is by looking at its URL. A spoofed website will often have a similar URL as the website it is copying. But the fake URL might have an extra letter. Other fake URLs use alternative spellings. Paying attention to these details can help people spot unreliable websites.

CHATBOTS

Chatbots are computer programs that can talk to people. Many use artificial intelligence (AI) to have humanlike conversations. People can use chatbots to quickly look up information. They can ask chatbots questions. They can ask chatbots to summarize data. The computer programs use huge amounts of data to decide how to answer the user.

Chatbots can be easy ways to find answers. But they are not always accurate. People should not use chatbots as sources. Chatbots find information from all over

Artificial Intelligence

Artificial intelligence is the science of making machines that do complex tasks that only humans used to be able to do. These tasks include writing and processing large amounts of data. Some people use AI to spread disinformation. AI technology is advancing quickly. Lawmakers are having a hard time keeping up. There are few laws regulating what AI can do.

the internet. They compile the information.
Then they use it to build answers. But much
of the information they use is incorrect.
These mistakes are called hallucinations.
ChatGPT is one of the most popular
AI chatbots. But a 2024 study found that

Every week, more than 100 million people use ChatGPT.

it provided misinformation more than 50 percent of the time.

Chatbots are also often biased. This is because the programs' information is taken from biased sources. ChatGPT has been shown to be racially biased. Some of the information it finds is racist. It repeats the information to the user. This can spread misinformation and bias.

Chatbots are not reliable sources. But they can be useful. People can use chatbots to aid in their research. Chatbots can suggest relevant papers or books. They can even help brainstorm ideas.

DEEPFAKES

Images and videos can be good sources of information. They can be used as primary sources. But advances in technology have made some images unreliable. Images and videos can now be easily created or changed using AI. The new material is called a deepfake. Deepfakes can show people doing things they never did. They can make a person look or sound like someone else. They can make new artworks in a specific artist's style.

    Some people use deepfakes for innocent purposes. But others use deepfakes to spread disinformation. According to the University of Virginia,

> On a small scale, deepfakers can . . . create personalized videos that appear to show a relative asking for a large sum of money to help them out of

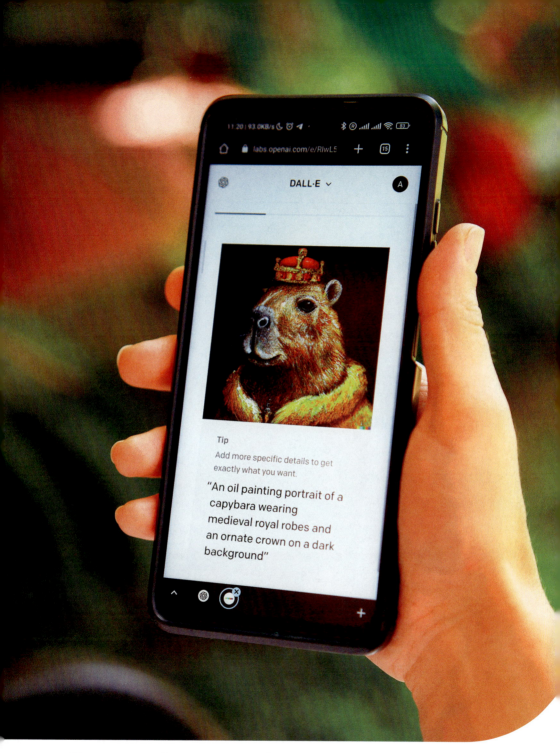

AI programs that can create images or can write are called generative AI programs.

In 2023, half a million deepfakes were shared on social media.

an emergency. . . . On a large scale, fake videos of important world leaders stating made-up claims could incite violence and even war.[8]

Signs that a video might be a deepfake include the person in the video blinking too much or too little. AI also has difficulty making realistic faces. Deepfake images of people might have unnatural facial expressions. The lighting on the face might not match the surroundings. The face might be blurry. The space between the face and the body might be blurry too.

CHAPTER FOUR

PUTTING SOURCES TO THE TEST

People should not trust everything they read or see. They should first evaluate the source the information is coming from. One way to do this is by using the SIFT test.

The SIFT test has four steps. Each letter stands for a different step. The test encourages people to stop, investigate, find better coverage, and trace claims, quotes, and media back to the original context. If a source passes each step of the test, people

People should always perform the SIFT test before sharing information with others.

Digital literacy expert Mike Caulfield created the SIFT test.

can generally trust the information that the source provides.

STOP

The first letter of the SIFT test stands for *Stop*. People should not trust everything they see. Some of the information might be false.

People should stop and think about a source before trusting its information. Is the source familiar? Is it reputable? If people are not sure, they should move on to the next step.

INVESTIGATE

The second letter of the SIFT test stands for *Investigate the Source*. People should do research about a source before trusting the source's information. One easy way to do this is by putting the name of the source into a search engine. This allows people to read about the source.

Wikipedia can be a great starting point for reading about sources. But anyone can edit a Wikipedia article. This means it is important to fact-check any information that seems suspicious. Wikipedia makes this easy. Each fact in a Wikipedia article is cited. This means there is a link next to each fact that shows where the information came from. People can click these links to verify the information in the article. The information should not be trusted if it does not have a citation. It should also not be trusted if the citation comes from an unreliable source.

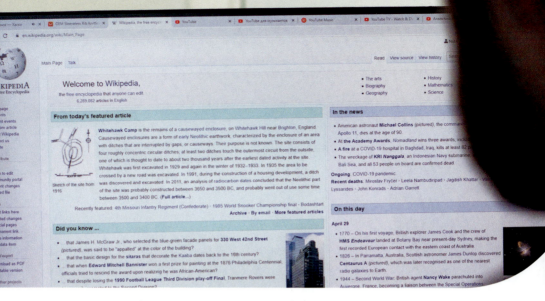

Some studies have found that Wikipedia is as accurate as or more accurate than traditional encyclopedias.

There are specific questions readers should be asking when investigating a source. Who created the source? Are they experts in their field? What credentials do they have? Why did they create the content? Answering these questions can help people decide if a source is reliable.

FIND BETTER COVERAGE

The third letter of the SIFT test stands for *Find Better Coverage*. Some sources

51

Search engines such as Google can help trace quotes back to their original context.

are not easily searchable. A friend might post information on social media. Or a family member might make a suspicious claim. People can look elsewhere when a source is not verifiable. They can search the information online. If the information is true, reliable sources have likely written about it.

Fact-checking websites can be great places to verify viral stories. These websites research whether rumors are true. Snopes is one such website. It rates the validity of different claims. Some claims are rated true or false. Others are rated somewhere in between. The website explains how it arrived at that ranking. Snopes also provides links to the sources it used to make the determination.

TRACE CLAIMS, QUOTES, AND MEDIA BACK TO THE ORIGINAL CONTEXT

The final letter of the SIFT test stands for *Trace Claims, Quotes, and Media back to the Original Context.* A friend may post an article online. But the friend is not the original source of the article. The person or company who originally wrote the article is the source. This is the source that should be evaluated.

Finding the original source of information can also help people better understand the whole story. Sometimes quotes are taken out of context. This can change how they are interpreted. For example, a newspaper reviewed a play based on the popular book *To Kill a Mockingbird*. The play used part of the newspaper's review as advertising. It quoted the paper as calling the play, "One of the richest experiences of my life."[9] However, this was not the full quote. The reviewer had actually written, "Reading this novel as a child was one of the richest experiences of my life. What a tragedy to see it ruined on stage."[10] Context can greatly change how information is interpreted.

Reverse Image Search

People can perform reverse image searches to find where images originally came from. This can help people see who posted images. It allows people to see the image's context. People can use Google Images to perform a reverse image search. A website called TinEye performs the same function.

MEDIA LITERACY MATTERS

Misinformation is everywhere. But media literacy can help people separate truth from fiction. People can use media literacy tools to ensure that sources are reputable.

Lee Krähenbühl teaches communications at Stevenson University. He believes that everyone should have strong media literacy skills. He says,

> Whether you are a journalist, researcher, writer, or someone in the professional fields, it is important to know how to identify real information and use it accurately. That's our real challenge in the twenty-first century.[11]

Media literacy skills can help everyone in their daily lives.

GLOSSARY

analyze
to examine carefully

authority
experience or knowledge

bias
favoring one idea, person, or group above others

consolidation
a combination of multiple things into a new, unified whole

conspiracy theorists
people who believe that an important secret is being kept from the public, often without proof

credentials
accomplishments that prove someone has experience or knowledge

malware
computer programs designed to damage a device or steal data

reputable
trustworthy or reliable

validity
accuracy

SOURCE NOTES

INTRODUCTION: A MOON LANDING CONSPIRACY?

1. Quoted in "One Giant Slip in Bangladesh News," *BBC*, September 4, 2009. http://news.bbc.co.uk.

2. Quoted in "One Giant Slip in Bangladesh News."

3. Amanda Ruggeri, "The 'SIFT' Strategy: A Four-step Method for Spotting Misinformation," *BBC*, May 10, 2024. http://news.bbc.co.uk.

CHAPTER ONE: FALSE INFORMATION

4. Heather Kelly, "How to Avoid Falling for Misinformation and Conspiracy Theories," *Washington Post*, July 15, 2024. www.washingtonpost.com.

5. Quoted in Kirsten Weir, "This Election Year, Fighting Misinformation Is Messier and More Important than Ever," *American Psychological Association*, January 1, 2024. www.apa.org.

CHAPTER TWO: SOURCES OF INFORMATION

6. Jenny L. Presnell, *The Information-Literate Historian: A Guide to Research for History Students*, 3rd ed., Oxford University, 2018.

CHAPTER THREE: SPOTTING UNRELIABLE SOURCES

7. Kelly, "How to Avoid Falling for Misinformation and Conspiracy Theories."

8. "What the Heck Is a Deepfake?" *University of Virginia*, n.d. http://security.virginia.edu.

CHAPTER FOUR: PUTTING SOURCES TO THE TEST

9. Quoted in David Lister, "David Lister: The Week in Arts," *Independent*, July 29, 2006. www.independent.co.uk.

10. Quoted in Lister, "David Lister: The Week in Arts."

11. Quoted in "How to Identify Reliable Information," *Stevenson University Online*, n.d. www.stevenson.edu.

FOR FURTHER RESEARCH

BOOKS

A. W. Buckey. *Legitimate News Sources*. San Diego, CA: BrightPoint Press, 2022.

Cindy L. Otis. *True or False: A CIA Analyst's Guide to Spotting Fake News*. New York: Feiwel & Friends, 2020.

Marne Ventura. *How to Identify Online Scams and Predators*. San Diego, CA: BrightPoint Press, 2025.

INTERNET SOURCES

"Media Literacy," *Crash Course*, 2018. https://thecrashcourse.com.

"SIFT Method of Evaluating Resources," *Northeast Wisconsin Technical College*, n.d. https://nwtc.libguides.com.

"Tips," *Be Media Smart*, 2023. www.bemediasmart.ie/tips/.

WEBSITES

PolitiFact
www.politifact.com

PolitiFact is an award-winning, nonpartisan fact-checking website. The organization evaluates the validity of viral claims. Its website allows users to search for specific claims and to browse claims by politician or topic.

Purdue Online Writing Lab
http://owl.purdue.edu

Founded by Purdue University, the Purdue Online Writing Lab contains resources for students conducting research. Its "Conducting Research" tab provides information on finding reliable sources. It also explains how to evaluate unfamiliar sources.

Snopes
www.snopes.com

Founded in 1994, Snopes fact-checks claims from politicians, viral social media posts, and urban legends. It also allows users to submit claims for Snopes to evaluate. Its "Quiz" tab tests users on their knowledge of false information.

INDEX

Armstrong, Neil, 6–9
artificial intelligence, 38, 39

chatbots, 38–41
confirmation bias, 14
COVID-19, 17–19

deepfakes, 41–45
disinformation, 12–16, 39, 42–45

Google Images, 55

Information-Literate Historian, The, 24

Kelly, Heather, 15–16, 35
Khan, Hasanuzzaman, 9
Krähenbühl, Lee, 56

misinformation, 12, 14, 18–19, 41, 56

newspapers, 6–9, 10, 54–55

Pennycook, Gordon, 19
primary sources, 20–25, 27, 29, 31, 41–42

Ruggeri, Amanda, 11

satire, 8–9
scams, 36
search engines, 50
secondary sources, 20–23, 25–27, 31
SIFT test, 46–55
Snopes, 53
social media, 11, 16, 17, 18, 53

tertiary sources, 20–23, 27–28, 31
TinEye, 55

websites, 8–9, 35–38, 53, 55
Wikipedia, 50

IMAGE CREDITS

Cover: © mediaphotos/iStockphoto
5: © oatawa/Shutterstock Images
7: © NASA
8: © Casey Bisson/Flickr
10: © Backgroundy/Shutterstock Images
13: © 13_Phunkod/Shutterstock Images
15: © GaudiLab/Shutterstock Images
17: © Red Line Editorial
18: © Studio Romantic/Shutterstock Images
21: © Samuel Borges Photography/Shutterstock Images
22: © Anne Frank Stichting, Amsterdam
25: © Uark Theatre
29: © TuiPhotoengineer/iStockphoto
30: © Clovera/iStockphoto
33: © fizkes/Shutterstock Images
34: © Zack Frank/Shutterstock Images
37: © Tero Vesalainen/Shutterstock Images
40: © Ascannio/Shutterstock Images
43: © Artie Medvedev/Shutterstock Images
44: © Tero Vesalainen/Shutterstock Images
47: © Ground Picture/Shutterstock Images
48: © Alan Levine/Flickr
51: © Postmodern Studio/Shutterstock Images
52: © Thaspol Sangsee/Shutterstock Images
57: © LightField Studios/Shutterstock Images

ABOUT THE AUTHOR

Heather C. Hudak has been writing and editing educational materials for more than twenty-five years. She has written hundreds of books for schools and libraries on all kinds of topics, including animals, technology, science, and history. When she is not writing, Heather enjoys traveling. She has been to more than sixty countries. She also enjoys spending time with her many cats and dogs.